Letting Go ...
with a Clenched Fist

NOREEN KAUFFMAN FENTON

WESTBOW
PRESS®
A DIVISION OF THOMAS NELSON
& ZONDERVAN

WestBow Press books may be ordered through booksellers or by contacting:

WestBow Press
A Division of Thomas Nelson & Zondervan
1663 Liberty Drive
Bloomington, IN 47403
www.westbowpress.com
844-714-3454

Scriptures taken from the Holy Bible, New International Version®, NIV®. Copyright © 1973, 1978, 1984, 2011 by Biblica, Inc.™ Used by permission of Zondervan. All rights reserved worldwide. www.zondervan.com The "NIV" and "New International Version" are trademarks registered in the United States Patent and Trademark Office by Biblica, Inc.®

ISBN: 978-1-6642-5055-0 (sc)
ISBN: 978-1-6642-5056-7 (e)

Library of Congress Control Number: 2021923537

Print information available on the last page.

WestBow Press rev. date: 12/8/2021

Dedicated to my mom, Lee Kauffman (1924–2020),
Who always told me I should write a book,
and who will now read it with new heavenly eyes.
And to my dad, Derald Kauffman (1921–2003),
Who gave me the drive to never quit
and finish what is started.
Your love and legacy run ribbons through every page of my story.

CONTENTS

ACKNOWLEDGMENTS

S O MANY PEOPLE HAVE BELIEVED IN ME AND THIS BOOK FOR SO MANY YEARS that it's impossible to list everyone, but some have risen to the top.

Ed Fenton. You have walked this journey with me for the last ten years. Thank you for understanding the dream of completing this, and for putting up with piles of paper, changing deadlines, and other parts of life being put on hold. Your prayers, support, love, and encouragement as my husband, partner, and friend have helped me cross the finish line, and I'm so thankful for you every single day. Love you beyond words.

Matt and Tony. As my sons, you are more a part of my story than anyone else. First as my babies, and now as grown men, you are the heartbeat of my "why" in life. Being your mom has kept me going through so many things I wasn't sure I would or could survive. Thank you for your love, your patience, and your forgiveness of this very imperfect momma. I love you.

Alaina, Kayla, Caleb, Nicole, Emily, Hudson, Warner, Tucker, Eden, Colton, Hayden, Miles, and Max. Being your stepmom, mom-in-law, future mom-in-law, grandma, and step-grandma has opened a whole new world to me! You are my tribe, and I love each of you more than I can say.

Marsha, Wanda, Chris, Penny, Connie, Anne, LeAnne, Christine, Cathy V., Cathy C., Cathie, Gay, Vickie, Karen, Jacque, Jill, and Janet. My girls—from friendships of ten to fifty-plus years, in different towns and states. Thanks for your prayers, listening ears, belief in me, sharing tears and laughter, and going through the letting go processes in my life events, even as this book has been written. Your friendships are gems in the treasure box of my heart.

Roger, Ray and Sally, Jim and Sharman, Rosie W., Joyce W., Mike and Joyce, Mona and George, Sheryl V., Pastor Joe, Deidre, Christy, the TBS gals, Chelle, Amy and Greg, Pam and Gregg, Brad and Christine, Pick, our Home Group, and all the others who took this dream seriously enough to continue to pray for me while I've been learning to live out this message. Thank you for your continual prayers, love, and support, especially when I was at my weakest. I couldn't have done it without you.

PROLOGUE

W HEN I FIRST BEGAN TO PUT THESE THOUGHTS ONTO PAPER, IT WAS A few years before the year 2020. And it is now 2021, a year after our world has been changed in every aspect by COVID-19. I don't know anyone who hasn't had to let go of something or someone in ways they never would have imagined before the pandemic. And the title I chose for this book was also something that came to me several years before a clenched fist would become a symbol of racial upheaval in the USA. There were so many times that I had to put this work down, due to medical issues, deaths of loved ones, and other major life events. At times, it would have been easier to throw in the towel.

But thanks to the prayers of faithful friends and family, and the grace and faithfulness of God, I now know that this is the very time for this message to be shared. A year ago, we had no concept of how many millions of people would be infected, and how many of those millions would die from the COVID virus. No one could have told us that our children would not be able to go to school, or that we would not be able to see our families and friends in social gatherings, or that we would lose our elderly loved ones without being able to be with them. A year ago, most of us believed that this would be a temporary inconvenience, at best, and maybe last a few months at worst. But our lives have been forever altered in ways we are still waiting to see the full effect of, and making it through nearly two years now seems to somehow mark a milestone that we are wearily acknowledging as a triumph. It's as though we've all been running this marathon together, yet apart, and are crossing what we hope is the finish line, and yet not sure if this race is ever going to end.

In the past few months, vaccinations have begun to be given to millions of people, and a feeling of hope is starting to permeate the world, with restaurants and stores opening back up, and families and friends slowly gathering again.

There are other times in life that can affect us in a similar way to how the pandemic has made us all feel. Broadsided by the unexpected and sometimes unimaginable. These times result in having to let go in ways we don't want to and perhaps are not sure we can survive. I am a fellow traveler on that journey and hope that this book can give you hope and encouragement that you are not alone in whatever you or a loved one is having to let go of. A loving Creator is ready to lead you to life and hope opening again. Will you grasp His hand?

CHAPTER 1

I Haven't Got Time
for the Pain

PAIN IS NO FUN. WHETHER IT IS PHYSICAL, EMOTIONAL, RELATIONAL, OR spiritual, the amount of time and effort it takes to heal is usually much longer than we want it to be. I went through a period of dealing with healing in all those areas, one after another. After a sudden fall on concrete, the loss of sleep from chronic pain caused a catch-22 cycle. I was trying to recover while still hurting too much to create an exercise routine that would help me get back into shape and sleep better. The emotional losses were just as great. Because of the pain, I had to give up a part-time job I loved and babysitting my grandson, whom I had been with weekly since he was six weeks old.

Shortly after falling, my sister and I moved our ninety-year-old mother from the familiarity of a town she had lived in for fifty-one years into a retirement home. Packing boxes and moving was awfully familiar to me, but the push of doing it in excruciating pain and exhaustion took its toll. Accomplishing the move in six weeks, with the two of us trying to figure out what to keep and what to sell, give away, or move, was not an easy task. And all the while, we were concerned for Mom's well-being and adjustment. We were also dealing with the loss of a place we had called home for decades.

Then in the middle of those dynamics, my faithful and loyal dog, who was my companion and buddy, died suddenly of a rare brain tumor. Helping with Mom's move had prevented me from taking Hazard for our regular walks, and I finally got to do that one afternoon. The next morning, I witnessed him having a horrible seizure. We rushed him to a vet hospital an hour away. He passed away before evening. I just wasn't ready for that loss too! Many tears were shed over the next few days, but I had to get right back to the traveling and packing required to finish Mom's move.

The packing process took longer than normal because of the debilitating pain I was still dealing with, as well as traveling the two-and-a-half-hour round trip to where she lived. When the move was finally finished, I felt I could breathe again and maybe get back to some sense of normal. The weather was still nice enough in late October to take a walk, so two days later I did. It was so difficult to take those first steps without Hazard, but I knew I needed to make myself go. Walking was always my way of unwinding and getting exercise, while praying, thinking, and enjoying the beauty of God's creation. We lived in the country, so the route I had taken for over three years with my dog was familiar and welcome on that day of recovery and rejuvenation.

As I headed home, I saw him out of the corner of my eye—a large, black dog on my side of the road. No owner around—no one else around. I was perhaps the length of a block away, painfully aware of not having my companion and protector with me. The dog was not leaving the area, and I needed to pass him to get home. I got closer, slowing down, reassuring myself that it would be okay because he was a big German shepherd, and my dog had been part shepherd. Still no owner in sight, so I knew caution was in order. It happened so quickly! Slowing down, I saw the look in his eye. I told him to go on home, and I walked past him. Then I sensed a quick movement from behind. It was an instant pain, a piercing in the back of my upper leg—and the shock of being bitten. But he did not leave. He crouched, with gritted teeth and a look that made me know I was still in trouble.

I stopped and stared back at him. Talking gently to him, I hoped soothing words would pacify any potentiality of him lunging again. My heart was pounding, my fear was rising, and I was paralyzed in place.

No one was around. My cell phone in hand, the call to my husband was quick and frantic. "Come get me, I'm in trouble. I've been bitten!" I was bleeding; the dog was not leaving, and I was not moving except for my head. I was looking frantically for an owner. It turned out that he was across the road behind his house, at least a hundred yards away, trimming trees with a power saw, oblivious that his dog had been gone for several minutes ... until he turned around. I was calling and waving to him, limping very slowly across the road, with his dog walking right next to me.

When the owner called his name, he finally broke into a run. My husband was on the way, and I was beginning to shake. As the owner came toward me, he strained to hear me call, "Your dog bit me!" several times, before he was close enough to hear. He was in disbelief that I had been bitten. I started crying, showing him my wounds and looking for my husband. He pulled up while I was getting the owner's name and number, and we quickly drove home. By the time the sheriff's officer showed up, the evidence of the bites was clearly visible on my leg. And the pain had begun. We told the officer what happened while she filled out the report. Next was a trip to the ER, involving three hours of waiting, examination, retelling the story, and then rabies shots, just to be safe. The twenty-one shots brought on a new level of pain. They were administered directly into the wound areas, surrounded by already-injured muscles still healing from me falling months before.

It was just too much, too close together, and nothing seemed to make sense. Why did I have to fall? Why did my dog have to die while I was saying goodbye to my childhood home? And then the dog attack—right when I was trying to get back to normal! I knew God was in control, and I tried hard to cling to scripture and people's encouragement, but the losses created a tsunami of emotions that ended up in some posttraumatic stress. I got discouraged from not being able to do simple tasks around the house without feeling stabbing pain up my arms, in my hip, and in my back.

It took five months before I could sleep in a bed, due to how hard it was to roll over or get comfortable. And I really, really missed my dog. He had been with me through some tough years, and he was a source of comfort through other losses. Several years before meeting my husband,

I had gone through a divorce and was raising my two sons. As they got older, they chose to live with their dad for longer periods of time. Hazard was there for me. He was there when my dad died, seeming to sense my grief. He greeted me at the door when the house got so very quiet after active teenaged boys moved away to college. And he was there, riding next to me in the front seat of the moving truck, when my big adventure of moving to Colorado ended, and we drove home. Even though my life had taken such a good turn with a new marriage and a wonderful husband, the gap of losing my dog took a long time to close. My discouragement and grief process were growing as fast as the pounds on the scale from inactivity, and everything just started seeming so hard. My prayers were centered around asking for strength, while I wondered if I'd ever get to take long walks again or mount our motorcycle. It took time—three years of it—but those things slowly became possible again.

I would have loved for it to take just a few months, but it didn't. In our hurried world, taking time for loss and grief seems abnormal. If I had been in a body cast, people would have been able to better understand why I wasn't acting like myself. But broken bones can heal faster than injured tissue, and I had only a very swollen wrist for anyone to see that I had been hurt at all. Isn't it that way with our hearts as well? When we go through pain that causes a broken heart, people don't always understand how long it can take to heal because they cannot see the wounds. In loss or grief, oftentimes well-meaning phrases are uttered, so the hurting person can be "fixed," when what is really needed is someone to walk beside him or her during the journey. It usually takes much longer than any of us are comfortable with.

The only one who truly knows the soothing balm we need is the one who also went through pain. His pain came from carrying a huge wooden cross on a beaten body. It came from having stakes driven through His hands to hold Him onto the cross while it slammed down into the ground. And it also came from wondering why it all had to happen that way. His heart was also broken—from all of us for whom He died. So many do not understand that He did all of that for us. That kind of love doesn't make sense to us. But it is that love we can hold onto amid our own pain. When others leave or just do not understand, He is still there. We can rest in the palm of His nail-scarred hands, knowing that He will carry us through to the necessary healing.

When I remember what He did for me, and that He understood a level of pain so much greater than mine, it helps me continue my own healing process. When I feel so alone in my pain, I remember that Jesus's best friends left Him alone in His most vulnerable times. One even betrayed Him to the soldiers who would kill Him. And on the days when the healing feels like two steps forward and three steps back, the words of scripture remind me to trust in God and not lean on my own understanding. And day by day, week by week, my hand clinging to His, healing comes. Sometimes it just takes time.

CHAPTER 2

Letting Go of Normal

WHEN OUR NORMAL IS DISRUPTED AND MAYBE CHANGED FOREVER, IT can feel like holding on to a merry-go-round that you know will eventually stop, but you don't know when, and holding on is the only thing you can do. And you hope you can have the strength to do that, without falling off! My normal has been changed many times. I thought my first marriage would be solid and secure, based on love and trust. I had no idea that a few years later I would be dealing with shattered dreams, a broken heart, and divorce. My new normal included balancing full-time work and raising two active boys for the next ten years. There were also new homes, new jobs, and the loss of a parent, among other changes. Then there were some years of being a single, middle-aged woman trying to navigate the dating world, which was much different and much scarier than decades before. Eventually, the new normal led to a wonderful man and new marriage, with a larger blended family and the joy of grandchildren. But the process of getting there included countless overwhelming days and lonely nights, full of prayer and questions about whether normal would ever include marriage again, or if I were to remain single. My normal began to change with every life change, and I finally have realized that even now, normal is more a setting on a dryer than the reality of life!

Sometimes, letting go of normal means releasing what has always been comfortable or familiar and trusting that God, the creator of the universe, just might have a plan that we wouldn't have picked ourselves, but one that will eventually bring unexpected peace and joy. Even when that new plan is a result of bad choices by us or someone else, those detours of life do not have to thwart the master plan of God to give us a hope and a future. But that often means letting go of holding on to what we knew and opening our hand to hold onto God's as we cross over into what is next. That cannot happen when we clench our fist in anger, unbelief, or control. It can only happen when we trust, opening one finger at a time, until our hand is outstretched to welcome God's. It is much easier, I have found from painful experience, to open my own hand up. In times that I didn't, my fingers were pried open through circumstances that were not in my control anyway, until I finally became too tired to hold on to my illusion of control and wearily reached out for a hand of help. No matter what, God's hand is there, waiting for ours to reach out to His and trust Him with the new normal that is in store for us.

One of my favorite times with our oldest grandson was when he was 2½ years old, and came to me, reaching up to be held. No matter what I was doing, reaching down and picking him up was the priority, even if it was just for a hug or to get another drink out of the frig, before he went on his busy way. The warm feeling that brought was insatiable because I wanted him to know how much I loved him and how eager I was to show it, by helping him or just loving on him! I imagine that's what God waits for us to do—just come to Him, putting our phones, computers, cars, schedules, and tablets down—and let Him meet our needs and our cries for help; then He watches us go our busy way. He is eager to show us how much He loves us, especially when our circumstances are spinning "normal" right out the window! But it cannot happen if we don't come to Him, and that is sometimes the last thing we do. For some reason, it seems to be part of our normal to try to fix whatever is going on around us, in us, or in someone we know. So, we cling, fists tightly clenched, to our very human, very fallible agenda, believing we just somehow know better than the One who "knit me together in my mother's womb"

(Psalm 139:13 NIV). It's as bizarre as my grandson thinking he knew more than Grandma about what he really needed. He may have *wanted* a cookie, but I knew that what he needed was some fruit and a good nap, whether he agreed or not! There were also times when he let me know in no uncertain way that he did *not* want me to help him do something. His little forefinger pointed at me, while he said "No, no, no, Gamma—*me* do it!" Then, when the toy didn't work, or he couldn't open something, or he couldn't get that one piece of food on his fork, he finally looked at me and said, "Gamma do it?"

We are like that with God—finally admitting that letting go means asking Him for help, with our exasperated prayers of "Lord, please handle this. I finally realize that I can't!" For us type A do-it-yourselfers, this admission is not easy. In fact, the words almost make us choke, because we have somehow equated asking God for help with weakness or failure. Or perhaps in certain circles, even Christian ones, we have been fed the lie of "God doesn't give you more than you can handle." I beg to differ! The Bible is full of stories of people going through way more than they can handle, and for that reason, falling on their knees or faces, begging God to rescue, forgive, or protect them, acknowledging the need for a perfect, all-loving, all-knowing Savior who can be trusted to handle it all! In fact, that's why Jesus had to be sent to this imperfect world to die for us imperfect, sinful humans, because we couldn't ever "get it right" without Him and the sacrifice of His life. We couldn't "handle" our own ability to follow a holy and perfect God, without a holy and perfect Savior.

Maybe you can relate, and maybe you are, or have been, going through a time of change that seems foreign to everything you know as being "normal." I want to encourage you that God has got this! Nothing takes Him by surprise, and He loves you right in the middle of the mess! He is waiting for you to walk, run, or crawl to Him, and is ready to scoop you up when you reach for Him. But He cannot do it until you let go of what you're clinging so tightly to. Nothing you are clinging to is as great as His love for you, and nothing is worth telling Him, "No, no, no," because His love and care for you are immeasurable. It doesn't matter how angry you are, how rebellious you are, how hurt you are, or how confused you are. Once you let go and hold onto Him, the new normal you will experience will include grace, peace, forgiveness, and healing. And *that* is worth holding on to! I continue to learn this lesson, because of finding out that letting go is a journey and a process and seems to be the theme of my life! After more than fifty years of being a Jesus follower, I'm still finding out that letting go of my tight grip on my plans, my relationships, my pain and disappointments, and even my own health, means gripping the hand of God and trusting Him to "do it," just like my little grandson trusted me. And as hard as the journey is at times, it always works out so much better when I quit clenching my fist and just relax in His grip!

CHAPTER 3

Letting Go of
Disappointment

I CAME TO GET AWAY—A MUCH-NEEDED BREAK FROM THE COLD AND DREARY Midwest weather, as well as a series of events through the last eight months that drained me physically and emotionally. All I wanted was a break from being cold, healing for an aching body due to recovering from serious injuries, and a way to let the ocean roll away the worries that had been plaguing me.

The challenges started on the first lap of the plane trip. I had carefully packed, so as not to have too heavy of a suitcase pulling on my still-weak wrist. Sleep had been short and sweet the night before leaving, due to the extensive list that needed to be accomplished before my "great escape," which was already affected by a sudden trip to a town an hour away to retrieve a lost wrist brace. I could not go without the brace, because the increased risk of deeper injury was far greater than the loss of time on the highway. So, leaving by 7:00 a.m. to catch a 9:16 flight was paramount, and I thought my biggest challenge was over. I just needed to get on that plane and head south for sun, ocean, and rest!

At the airport, all was smooth, and I was elated! My sweet husband had dropped me off, staying behind to meet the demands of work that prevented the possibility of him accompanying me. I got to breeze through security with a special pass and didn't even have to remove my shoes. The grin on my face must have been palatable, as the joy and anticipation of being on a beach in a few hours pushed back the reality of being in twenty-five degrees for the last time, for at least four days! Then I got to the sign. You know, the sign on the board saying the flight had been delayed due to ice (for some reason we were heading north to end up in the south). It seems that the Minneapolis area had a huge snow and ice storm, and the plane coming in was delayed just enough to create a problem in getting to the connecting flight in time, once I would land there. The agent at the desk was nice but business-like, while she hastily punched the computer buttons with the well-known style of someone who knew they couldn't give me good news. No other flight was going to that area of Texas that day. The choice was take a risk and try it—knowing that getting to Minneapolis meant the possibility of having to stay in the airport overnight—or wait till the next day. I knew the trip was important, and I knew God was in it. I promptly texted all the people in my life whom I knew would pray and decided to risk it. It seemed ironic—wanting to leave to rest and write about trusting the Lord with all that we have to let go of, and the first test of the day was getting to the destination to do that!

I took the risk and told a flight attendant on the plane about my dilemma, asking how far it was from gate to gate for the connecting flight once we would land, explaining that I was recovering from injuries, and just wasn't able to do the "airport dash" across the terminal. He ordered a cart for me to ride in, and I sat back in my seat, preparing to possibly spend the night in one of the coldest spots in the nation, instead of heading for one of the warmest ones. But when I got down to the busy concourse, no cart was in sight. My eyes dashed to-and-fro very quickly, while looking for directions to get to my next flight, and the decision was made quickly to not take the risk of waiting for the cart, because there was just no time to spare. My aching body and struggling emotions decided to go on autopilot, and I walked/ran as fast as my damaged muscles would go, gripping a carry-on tote that seemed heavier by the minute. My name was being announced when I was within earshot of the gate, and when I arrived, breathless and sweating (even in the cold), the gate attendants started clapping! Evidently, my demeanor and gasping announcement of "I'm here!" shocked them into being nice to me, instead of reprimanding my almost missed entry to the plane!

The rest of the flight was fine, and my arrival to southern Texas was more than welcome by the time some dear friends picked me up at the airport. The relief of arriving was monumental, and my mood quickly changed to relief and anticipation of sunshine, rest, and time to write. The first afternoon was slightly cloudy but warm enough to take a long walk on the beach, watching the long-awaited ebb and flow of crashing ocean waves and soaring seagulls. I knew that the next three days would be just *wonderful!* Sleep was welcome and came quickly that night—the best I had had in many months of painful nights in a recliner from a sore hip and wrist and lower back injuries. The next morning, I woke up rested and ready to see the sun. But the sun was not showing up. There were clouds, cool winds, and not many folks on the beach, but I was determined. After another long walk, and meeting friends for lunch, I bravely donned some shorts and lay in a chaise lounge on the beach, listening to the soothing waves and feeling very grateful to be there. By the time the evening sun was going down, the waves were much bigger, the winds much stronger, and the temperature had dropped about twenty-five degrees. As night progressed, the winds were so strong that hotel lawn chairs were sliding across the pool area, and busy hotel personnel were strapping down what they could and moving whatever was left. Winds pulled the waves high against the blackness of night, visible from my window. I was amazed at how the scene was so opposite of what I had been eagerly hoping for and looking forward to, but I finally went to sleep, believing the next day would bring relief from the unusual conditions for that area. The heater was on, and I crawled into a warm bed.

However, a few hours later, I awoke to feeling much colder, and realized the soothing sound of the heater fan had stopped. And so had everything else. There were no lights, and the room's temperature was going from cold to colder. The area around the heater was allowing cold wind to push into the room, so I covered it with an extra comforter from the bed and called the front desk. Yes, they were aware of the situation, and no, there was no power on my floor or several others, because the wind had knocked out the power lines! They said it was unusual weather for that time of year, and that it could be hours before power would be restored. The irony of once again being not only cold but also with no power, made my long-awaited retreat from the frigid Midwest rather like a bad joke! The morning sun brought relief as well as repair people, and eventually all power was back on. But I had to deal with disappointment—it just wasn't what I had planned on! I had planned to get away from tremendous stress coming from life-altering events of several months. The idea was to vegetate and be renewed by South Padre Island sun and waves, so that I could face the next stress of finishing getting my mom's one-hundred-plus-year-old home ready to put on the market. Instead, the get-away seemed to be plagued with its own set of stressors. I was trying to still be thankful, as I had been reminded to do through prayer and reading appropriate Bible verses. I *was* thankful to be there, but I had to be honest with myself in how let down I felt once again that I couldn't just relax and rest in the environment that I had hoped for—and somehow felt I deserved. I mean *really?* Instead of being soaked in warm, sunny rays by peaceful ocean breezes, I was sitting wrapped up in a bed comforter with no power, watching lawn chairs flying through the dark, with what seemed like hurricane-level waves! Not my idea of a calm, relaxing getaway, and once again, the tears came as I dealt with reality versus the pretrip fantasy that I had hung onto for a sense of relief. And with the tears came the prayers, as they had so many times before in life, when what I had hoped for did not measure up with what came to be.

My disappointment came from not having my expectations of what I thought I needed meet up with reality. Once I released my grip of not getting what I had hoped for, the trip turned out fine. Even though there wasn't much sun, I got to enjoy time with friends, rest, and even have a few warm-enough moments to sit on the beach and enjoy the ocean. I had to let go of what I wanted, to receive what I needed as still being just as big of a gift of God. That trip resulted in the area being a place of rest and relaxation that Ed and I have enjoyed on an annual basis for several years now, and we have also developed some wonderful friendships with people from all over the country who stay in the same condominium complex. And most of the time, the sun is out, and the beach is beautiful. You just never know when letting go of disappointment can open new and unexpected blessings!

CHAPTER 4

Letting Go of Expectations

SOMETIMES WHAT WE NEED IS RIGHT IN FRONT OF US; THAT HAS BEEN A tagline in so many movies! We get it. We're the people in the audience. We hold our breaths, as the plot agonizingly rolls into the story of the person who is looking for love in all the wrong places. After a tearful realization of yet another lover jilting her or him, the good and faithful friend is there for a shoulder to cry on. The music swells (it always swells right then), and as if a switch were suddenly flipped on, the jilted, or misdirected lover finally gets it! And he or she falls hopelessly in love with the one who was there waiting all along. Everyone who has watched one, or one hundred, of those movies, always holds their breath just a little bit, while the clash of expectations versus reality shows once again that real, honest, faithful, love is much better than an expectation that is not only an illusion, but usually very unhealthy in some form. Many of us have experienced a similar plot in real life—yours truly included.

I cannot help but wonder if that is why we often hold on to an expectation, and then feel so let down when it is not met. The scenarios are as endless as the availability of those types of movies. Someone you thought was a true friend deeply hurt you. A promotion that you sacrificed endless hours of work and sleep to earn, went to someone else. He lied to you. She cheated on you. The church leader made a poor decision that cost both his and the church's reputation. The financial investment that you were told was a sure thing, ended up costing your lifetime savings, and you just were not planning to work another ten years. You have discovered that your perfect little baby is not such a perfect teenager. You can almost hear the music swell, as the light goes on, and you finally get it! The part of your heart that's hurting so deeply is picked up and cradled by the only One who was there for you all along. He is the shoulder that you have cried on, begging for the relationship to work or the deal to go through. He was there waiting, as you continued to wrap your heart around an expectation that proved to not be true. He was the one holding you while you cried in the night, hearing your screams of "It's not *fair!*"

He knows. It probably wasn't fair. His life wasn't fair either. His family and friends didn't always believe who He was. His inner circle of friends, who traveled with Him for three years, betrayed Him, rejected Him, and some just wouldn't believe His power, even though they saw miracle after miracle being performed by Him. He was falsely accused, tortured, not given a fair trial, and killed in a brutal style reserved for the worst of criminals. And through it all, He never tried to escape or call on the thousands of angels whom He had the power to beckon for His protection and escape. He had to die for us, so that we could "get it"! He is the only One capable of meeting every expectation of our hearts that are truly always best for us! Can you hear the music swell? We can carry our dashed expectations, hurting hearts, ruined plans, and disillusionments to Him, the One who is always the faithful Friend, and feel the embrace of the One who will never leave us.

I have felt the deep fangs of betrayal, deception, and bewilderment, coming from imperfect human beings in some excruciating and life-altering ways. I did not expect to go through a divorce. I did not expect to be a single parent for ten years. I did not expect to lose a job. I know all too well the nights of soggy, tear-stained pillows, and of staring at a mindless TV screen when an exhausted mind and heart just wouldn't submit to sleep. I have experienced physical pain and health problems, and scars of broken promises toward myself and my loved ones. And every time, I have wondered if there are heavenly beings watching these scenarios, in the audience of my life, holding their breath, while the music swells, until I finally get it. None of those dashed expectations, things, or people could fill the place in my heart reserved for True Love. That love is always there, meeting every piece of my broken heart, with arms wrapped around me. Those arms that once were attached to a cross by only the muscles and flesh, and bones framing a jagged hole around a huge stake driven into each hand. And the music swells, and I finally turn around and see His face amid it, with eyes of compassion, and the same scarred hands catching every one of my tears. And I finally get it … it is true *love* … and He's been there all the time. His name is Jesus. He wipes my tears and smiles as my prayers of surrender, release, and forgiveness are uttered into His welcoming shoulder. And the heavenly angel audience sighs, as the music slowly fades, and the healing begins.

He is there for you and your life movie too. He is waiting for you to turn to Him as the One whom you can trust and be completely honest with, or maybe come back to, after a long and painful absence on your part. He has His arms open, and His hands are wet with your tears, because He's counted every one of them. And True Love is always, always better than the counterfeit of it. He knows you like no other because He created you! Nothing in your life movie surprises Him or shocks Him or makes His love be unavailable to you. He is the writer, director, and producer of your movie and has the best ending just waiting for you. Can you hear the music swell?

CHAPTER 5

Letting Go of the
Perfect Christmas

"THIS IS JUST A DIFFERENT KIND OF CHRISTMAS." I HAVE BEEN HEARING that a lot from people for the last couple of years. So many friends will have an empty chair for the first time at their tables, where someone they loved always sat, and they must decide how to cope with that. I have lived all those feelings and felt the heartache of knowing that Christmas would never be quite the same, and yet it had to continue to happen, for those of us still living. The feelings included an almost adamant determination to still make it beautiful and magical and full of love—and to picture a loved one celebrating Christmas for the first time in a place of no suffering or heartache or cancer or Parkinson's disease. The first Christmas after my dad died, there were tears, a group hug, and an extra surprise that brought more tears. He had evidently told my mom to give my two sons a special financial gift that I didn't know about. It was very generous, and much more than what they normally got at Christmas. We had been a single-parent household for six years by then, and to say the budget had been tight would be a major understatement. However, I always managed to give a good Christmas to the boys, wanting so desperately to somehow make up for the fact that the divorce meant their

Christmas would not be the same as before. It now included dividing time between two parents and two homes, and everyone, including my extended family, learning to adjust to that dynamic. Dad and I never talked about that, but he was very perceptive, and I'm sure he knew what motive my efforts came from. And he also knew during his last days in the hospital that year that the boys would be ages fifteen and eighteen on the first Christmas without him. The surprising and meaningful gift of a bigger sum of money would be a way for them to understand that he trusted them to use wisdom on how to spend it. Almost a message of letting them know he expected them to not only remember him that way, but that he knew they were becoming young men, and their choices with money and other things, were now up to them. Of course, our tears of loss turned to laughter, recognizing the fact that his way of spending it would have been to save it—for a rainy day!

That was my family's first different Christmas because of losing my dad. We had also had another different Christmas the first year after the divorce. The boys were eight and eleven, and I was facing having just gone back to work full time for the first time in twelve years. On top of that, because of how the settlement came out, their dad received the home we were living in, and I found a nice rental in the same school district to move the boys and I into, and their Christmas break was when that had to happen. We somehow managed, with the help of friends and family, to get moved in, have the tree decorated and in the new house, and have enough boxes unpacked to make it feel somewhat like home by Christmas. I was reeling with a broken heart, facing a new world of single-parenting, and incredibly determined to give the boys as good of a Christmas as possible. The gifts were still being wrapped into the wee hours of Christmas Eve and placed beautifully under the tree, so that the boys could wake up to that magical feeling. However, even buying a real tree, which had been the tradition, became an exercise of frustration and facing reality, as my boys tried to help me get it on top of the car, tied on well enough to make it home without causing a major traffic problem due to having it slide off while in transit! By the time I put it in the stand, saw how crooked it was, took it out of the stand, sawed it again, put it back in the stand, saw how crooked it *still* was, then finally collapsed in tears, I knew that Christmas just could not be the same, no matter how valiant my efforts were. The boys were in bed by then, and I was depleted physically, emotionally, and mentally. I had to come to a very stark realization—no matter what I would do to try to make their Christmas normal, it just couldn't be. It could be wonderful, but it would always be different from that point on. My tears and prayers continued into the night, begging God to give me the strength to go on and do whatever I could to always make Christmas as special as possible, even while accepting the stark differences. As the next ten Christmases rolled on, we all three got used to the new system. The boys, who were my parents' only grandchildren, would spend Christmas with me, waking up with the tree and gifts greeting them. We read the Christmas story from the Bible, while sipping on hot chocolate and a light breakfast, then tore into the gifts, some of which had only been wrapped a few hours by the time my exhausted body would drag into bed the night before. Later in the morning, my extended family would show up, and we'd have a ham dinner, then start with gifts again, always laughing about Dad's unique designs with the cash he would slip into the tree—sometimes it was a bow tie, sometimes a little house, all made out of bills that he carefully folded, as though to let us see his well-hidden creative side! Despite being exhausted from finishing everything up the night before, I always got a second wind of energy. My body and soul were fed by the laughter, fun, food, and most importantly the joy of seeing the boys smiling, yelling with joy over gifts, and enjoying extended family time. There was the traditional driving around to look at beautiful light displays, then heading home, so the boys could go to their dad's overnight and have another celebration with him. My extended family would stay a bit longer and then head to their respective homes out of town. And then I had to face again the loneliness of it being just me and the tree, piles of opened gifts, some dirty dishes, and the reality of private tears being a new part of Christmas. As time went on, it got easier, and Christmas night became a sort of spiritual reminder that the first Christmas was not perfect either.

Mary did not choose to have her holy baby born in a dirty, stinky manger—with complete strangers around! Joseph had not planned to go with plan B in trying to find a place for his family to stay. I'm sure he would have preferred that one of those inns would have had a vacancy sign on it! I'm thinking that Mary's mom was also struggling with not being able to be with her teenage daughter during such a momentous and challenging time of childbirth, especially with living through the last few months of gossip and whispers about how she got pregnant in the first place! And I'm also thinking that Mary's Dad might have been more than just a little upset at the whole situation, including Joseph dragging his daughter off away from him and the security and safety he had raised Mary in, up to that point. The very first Christmas had enough dysfunction in it to create a modern-day reality show, if you really think about it. And that is exactly why it had to happen that way. God knew that we humans would need a not-so-perfect Christmas to have as a model for our not-so-perfect lives. We somehow along the way substituted Norman Rockwell scenes for the reality of what Christmas really looked like from the beginning. God let His perfect Son be born in an incredibly imperfect setting rather than a palace, which is where other kings were usually born. This king of promise, king of hope, and king of our hearts came in an uncomfortable, unusual, and unprecedented way to an ungrateful, unbelieving world. There was nothing Norman Rockwell about that, or about the rest of His life. God knew that all these years later that would give us all hope, when our Christmases take on a different form and feel than what we want or have been used to.

My Christmases continue to change. After some hard and lonely ones, they are now filled with a big, blended family, lots more food, gifts, and laughter, a loving husband whom I'm thankful also loves Christmas, and the best part—grandkids! I still stay up way too late finishing things up on Christmas Eve, but there is still the wonderful, warm feeling of looking at the glowing tree, with all of the other lights out, packages wrapped beautifully, and the anticipation of smiles and laughter as each recipient will open them on Christmas Day. I've learned to blend traditions, meals, time, and expectations as our family continues to grow with adult kids and other families to share the day with. I'm also continuing to learn to let go of what I think Christmas Day "should be" and accept the changes each year brings, as well as accepting my own limitations that come with age and a much lower energy level than I used to have! And my heart still breaks, and I still shed private tears for those whom I know will be dealing with their first different Christmases. One especially hard year, it was loved ones who were dealing with cancer, the murder of a loving mom and grandma, a rebellious teenager whose choices affected the whole family, and the family who lost their twenty-two-year-old son to suicide in early December. And my prayer for them was to somehow be able to let go of what was their normal and grasp the hand of the God who created the first Christmas in what seemed to be a most abnormal place. And with tear-stained hands in His, we can all sit at the manger, look into the eyes of the baby, and still feel the wonder of hope and peace and joy, in the middle of our messy, imperfect lives. It's the only way I have seen people, including myself, be able to continue to truly celebrate life while dealing with major loss. Choosing getting better over getting bitter cannot happen with a fist that's clenched around what was. It can only happen with an open hand grasping the One who holds our future in His hands. He gave us Christmas to be more than just the "reason for the season." He gave it to us because His son was the most precious gift He could give, so we could open the gift of life and forgiveness—each imperfect day. And no matter what else we experience on and around December 25, *that* is what will always make it a perfect Christmas!

CHAPTER 6

Letting Go of Figuring
Out the Future

"It doesn't feel right," I said to my husband, Ed, on the phone. "I know," he said, "but it's the right way to go; just trust me." We were in two cars at one in the morning, driving on adrenaline and excitement, heading five hours from home to meet our new grandson, who had made his entrance into the world at 12:11 a.m. For scheduling reasons, I needed to leave about fifteen minutes behind Ed in my own vehicle, enabling my stay to last a little longer, helping the new mom and baby after their return home. In the wee hours of the morning, trying to save cell phone juice, which was rapidly depleting, I was relying on Ed's verbal directions at a certain turn, rather than what my phone GPS kept dictating. In the pitch-black Nebraska night, the thought of no cell phone service was a little unnerving, so making the correct turn took on a new importance! So, with the GPS lady's voice repeatedly telling me one thing, I chose to follow the voice I knew and trusted instead, and of course ended up on the very road I needed to be on! But the decision to follow his voice was not without internal (and a little verbal) conflict. The argument in my head went kind of like this: "What if he's wrong? Then I could be turned around in the wee hours of the morning with no company for miles, other than the occasional semi-truck flying by me! And I wanted Ed to get there as soon as possible to be with his daughter (my stepdaughter), so I didn't want to have to worry him if I got lost either. And my cell phone is on 20 percent! If I lose connection from too much GPS time, the worst scenario would be not being able to continue to contact Ed or follow any more directions to get rerouted, especially at such an early hour!" Then it hit me. He had just taken that turn half an hour before. He had already taken the path. I could happily ignore the irritating GPS lady and trust the one who had already gone before me on that route! Also, he was invested heavily in my decision. He explained that his route was much safer than what GPS was saying, because the highway was four lanes instead of two lanes, and it went more directly to the next city, which he knew I would prefer. He also didn't want me to go through unnecessary stress or problems when he knew my concern was cell phone coverage. And he wanted what I wanted—to see the darling newest member of the family as soon as possible!

Sometimes God's voice is the same for me. He already knows what is ahead in every decision I make, so when the other voices are shouting, "Do it this way! Buy this thing because you deserve it, or you can afford it! You don't need to forgive her; she was the one in the wrong! Go ahead and eat that. One little bite won't hurt you! You can say yes to one more commitment—after all, you can sleep when you're dead!" And the wrong directions go on and on. And amid all the voices, God's still, small voice whispers to me: "Trust me, my daughter. I won't mislead you. I love you, and I already know what is ahead of you. Trust me and do it my way. It will be better for you if you do. I have promised not to ever leave or forsake you, and your best is always in My plan for you!" Then the decision is up to me. Do I listen to the voice of the One who loves me and goes before me—or all the other voices that really have no investment in the outcome of my decisions? It seems so simple, and yet I can make it so incredibly hard! The listening is the first step; then comes the action part. Doing something about what we know to be true should be so easy, shouldn't it? And yet, there is that human struggle in all of us that has been a problem since Eve decided to ignore the voice of the Creator. Her decision to "play God" and choose her way, instead of listening to His loving voice of protection, created the beginning of the mess. Ever since then, humankind has struggled with thinking we somehow can hold onto doing things our own way, and we have also struggled with the huge cost of that decision over and over and over.

Since starting this book, the 2016 and 2020 presidential elections have come and gone, with a president from both the Republican and Democratic parties winning, and half of the USA being in an uproar. The outcome of Donald Trump's major win visibly shocked the media as well as all Americans who planned on Hillary Clinton becoming our next president. The outcome of Joe Biden's win was met with controversy and the eventual storming of the nation's capital on December 6, 2021. People were either elated or angry after each result, and there were resulting riots going on in parts of the country each time. Social media posts expressed every emotion, and many of us are just wanting to move on with life, putting the bitter and devisive months of election toxicity behind us. The country's brokenness has seemed to become a glaring reality during these last two elections, and no matter who the office of the commander in chief is occupied by, the truth of our nation's heart has been revealed. We are a divided, hurting, and angry group of citizens who need a healing that goes beyond an electoral process. Somewhere along the way, we quit listening to the voice of the God in whom our founding fathers trusted. We started taking another route, listening to other voices that seemed like a repetitive GPS lady convincing us to turn left when we should have turned right, just like the dark night I spent on the Nebraska roads when I just wanted to get to my destination and see my new grandson! Our nation has been in a slow boil of self-absorption, greed, and idolatry for many years, and it seems to be now boiling over with racial violence, hatred, and division that those of us my age have not seen the likes of since we were children, riding out the tail end of segregated schools and riots on college campuses. We have just wanted what we wanted, and it's all catching up with us. When we trust every other voice except the One who sent His son to die for us, and our security is focused on an elected official or a political party or the stock market, it's always going to be a wrong heart turn. And then comes the letdown of disappointment and disillusionment, because none of those things can save our hearts and souls, but instead they put a Band-Aid on something that needs surgery, which is our hearts.

The first of the Ten Commandments is to not have any idols before the Lord our God, and I'm convinced He told humankind that, because He knew that nothing or no one else would ever satisfy our hearts and souls the way He does! He gave that commandment because He loves us, not to spoil our fun! But He never forces us to do what He says. He lets us learn sometimes very painful lessons when we decide to not heed that commandment and try to replace Him with what we want when we want it, in the way we want it. And then when something goes wrong, or the results don't line up with our expectations, we seem to either get mad or get sad. And who is often the first to catch our blame? That's right, God—the one who tried to direct our paths for good in the first place. The loving heavenly Father who catches our tears and loves us enough to watch us fall flat on our pride, stubbornness, and self-will but is always there to pick us back up and give us another chance to listen to His voice next time. He just wants us to reach our destination with as few detours as possible, and He does not want us to get lost!

Years ago, I heard a saying that has stuck with me and helped me when I have most needed the reminder. That saying is: "There is a God, and it's not me!" Seems so simple, but every time I choose to go my own way or ignore what His words (by print or by spirit) say, I am forgetting this simple truth. I am not God; neither are you. We all are imperfect, fallible folks who love to somehow think we can live life on our own. Even those of us who say we believe in who He is and His wisdom and power can struggle with the "Eve complex" and basically tell the One who created us and the entire universe that "I've got this!" It is so much easier to see control issues in other people and miss our own. So, I continue to wonder where this deep need to control outcomes comes from. For some of us, it is from overcritical parents or childhood trauma or being hurt one too many times in relationships. Or for others of us, it's a pure motive of wanting to prevent hurt or heartache in loved ones' lives, so we jump in and try to "help," instead of trusting God with being big enough to handle taking care of them as well as taking care of us, as we watch the situation unfold. I'm learning that I need to *pray to be prepared* in those cases and not try to *precontrol the outcome!* That's hard for those of us who are "fixers" or are naturally gifted to want to help anyone we love to not go through what we see as unnecessary pain or circumstances that they might avoid if they just listened to us. But there is always a bigger picture that we cannot see, and oftentimes the very lesson that our loved one needs to learn would have been sabotaged if our well-meaning words of wisdom had been heeded. In praying for our loved ones, as well as in our own lives, it is good to be reminded to "Lean not on your own understanding, but in all your ways acknowledge Him (God), and He will direct your paths" (Proverbs 3:5–6 NIV).

The tears I shed for my friends and family members and the pain in their lives from difficult situations are but a mist in the huge teardrops of heavenly sorrow that I believe God experiences when we don't live life His way. He wanted us so badly that He gave Jesus for us, so that we would know He wants the best for us because it cost His perfect Son His life. The unfair torture, unjustified arrest, and unbelievable crucifixion came from no fault of His own, so that we could grasp the depth of God's love and the price He paid for us to trust Him and His ability to give us a future and a hope (Jeremiah 29:11 NIV). Those outstretched arms on the cross were holding every wrong decision, every act of selfishness, every hurtful thing we've said, every heartache, every misguided choice, every victim of abuse, and even every abuser who chooses to turn to Him in repentance and forgiveness. And His love never, ever quits. So, we can grab those hands with huge nail scars in them and let go of our own inability to figure out the future for ourselves and our loved ones and pray to be prepared as a far better plan unfolds!

CHAPTER 7

Letting Go of Shame

S HE WAS CAUGHT IN A LIFE OF SHAME AND HUMILIATION. HER PROFESSION was the way she survived, and yet it was killing her. Prostitution—let's call it what it was—was a lifestyle that created such isolation that she had to go to the community well early when no one else was there. She just did not want to deal with the pointing fingers and whispers again! All she wanted was to get some water without any drama. Then she would hurry home, with her head bowed, so she would not have to face the stares of disgust and shaking heads. Her plan was to slip out of the place she had stayed, get some water, and take a bath, so she could wash off the memories of the night before.

But before she could leave, they started coming—the men of the area—some with familiar faces—and bodies. And they were not going to leave her alone. The jeering eyes, the painful, accusing words, the self-righteous looks on their faces all felt like daggers into her soul. But the worst was the laughter, like they were being entertained at a party. She was their sick form of entertainment, and she couldn't just leave and go to the safety of her own home. Like attacking dogs, crouched and ready, their accusations of her uncleanness came flying, loud enough for others to hear, including the little children playing nearby. Then she saw the stones, clenched in hands ready to be hurled at her. Where was her escape? Where were they taking her? Panic gripped her heart as she realized they were dragging her to the temple courts, where everyone could see her. The humiliation and shame pushed her head low, as she felt them push her in front of someone, telling Him she was caught in adultery, and asking if she should be stoned.

Then she heard His voice—calming, peaceful, protective. Confronting the accusing men with their own sin, while slowly coming between her and them. Protection, peace, and relief were filling her heart, along with bewilderment. Who was this? How did He seem to know her with just one look, yet not the same kind of look that she knew all too well? The other men's looks were full of lust and loathing, all in one face. His look radiated a kind of love that was completely selfless, touching the depths of her pain-filled, used-up heart that had long since lost any hope of being protected and cherished. It was a look that made her feel embarrassed and exhilarated, cleansed and comforted, relieved and restored, all at once.

He also investigated the hearts of her accusers and told them whoever had no sin to throw the first stone at her. There was a hush over the crowd, and one by one, they left. And her life was changed forever. She gave up being used up by men, to follow Him and serve others. She was there with His disciples and mother, hearing Him preach, watching Him heal people in unbelievable ways. She ate and laughed with them as they all traveled together, being treated like a sister, instead of an object of pleasure. And her life, and her face, and her spirit were all transformed into something new and healed and whole. She *loved* this life! She could go to the well now to get water, head held high, even when the other women were there. The shame and guilt were gone! Life following Him was peaceful and good.

Then they arrested Him. Those soldiers, full of hate and brutality. She watched through the crowd as He was beaten in horrifying ways, while trying to comfort His sobbing mother. She knew the pain of being accused of what she had done, but they accused Him of things He had not even done! And He let them; He did not even fight. She knew He could make them go away, like He did for her that day at the well. Why didn't He? It was like He knew He had to let it all happen, and yet He had that same look of love in His eyes—even toward them. She could not understand or grasp what was happening; she just knew she couldn't leave. Even when those soldiers nailed His hands and feet to a rough wooden cross, and He was crying out in agony, she just couldn't leave. Then she watched Him die there, with soldiers mocking and laughing at Him (familiar sounds to her), while blood poured down His whole body in scarlet ribbons of pain. Things had happened so fast in the three days since He had been arrested that she could hardly breathe. Now He was dead, although He had told all His disciples that He would always be with them, she wondered what was happening, and how she would continue to live. But there wasn't time to think about it all. When Joseph took His limp body off that cross and put it in his private tomb, at least she knew she could touch Him one more time. Even though His body had been wrapped in oils and cloth, she just needed that last look.

It was Saturday evening, though, and she needed to wait because the Sabbath rest had begun. She welcomed the rest—one day to just sleep a little bit and try to let her exhausted heart and mind recover from the whirlwind of events. She had not had time to process the pain. It had all gone too fast, and her little bits of sleep that night were jolted with vivid nightmares of all that the last forty-eight hours had included. It was still so unbelievable! She just wished she could see His entombed body one more time, thinking it somehow would help. So, she got up early and went to the tomb. His mother, Mary, was there, and she wondered what it must be like to know that the little baby that momma bore thirty-three years before and swaddled so carefully would now be wrapped in strips of cloth used only for the dead. They got there, and something was wrong; the soldiers were gone. Those soldiers were ordered to stand guard all night so that the body could not be stolen by Jesus's followers. It was to squelch any chance of the rumor that Jesus would rise from the dead. That is what they had heard Him say would happen, and they didn't want to provide an opportunity for it to look that way. That guard group was specially chosen, with the clear orders that it could mean their own death if they allowed anyone to get close enough to steal the body. So, they had sealed the stone in front of the tomb and stood watch in front of it all day and night.

But the soldiers were nowhere to be found! And as the women

approached, they saw that the huge circular stone in front of the tomb was rolled away from the opening. What was happening?! She ran toward the opening, and carefully, slowly stepped in. Her eyes adjusted to the dim interior. She looked at the tablet of stone that was used to lay His body on, but there was no body! She couldn't breathe, her grief-stricken mind and heart began to reel, as she also realized that the strips of death-linen were lying on the stone tablet. Her legs gave out from under her, and she sank to her knees, with all the grief and unbelief of the whole weekend finally consuming her. The tears came in sobs—deep gut-wrenching sobs—as her mind tried to wrestle with the fact that she was not even able to see His body for the last time. Then she heard a voice, asking her why she was crying, and who she was looking for. Barely able to speak, she uttered, "Sir, if you have carried Him away, tell me where you put Him, and I will get Him" (John 20:15 NIV). She did not know how she would do it, but she just would. Then she heard that voice, the same one that had lifted her shame-filled face by the well those many months before. And hearing that voice, she felt it—the same flood of peace, hope, and joy as before! "Mary" (John 20:16 NIV). She turned in unbelief. It was Jesus! He was right there, right in front of her, saying her name, and all her pain and anguish melted away as she rushed toward Him. He told her not to touch Him, because He had not yet gone to His Father God in heaven. He also had a special job for her—to give a message to the men who had been with Him for three years. They were His twelve guys, whom He called His brothers. He told her to tell them that He was returning to "My father and your Father, to my God and your God" (John 20:17 NIV). So, she ran, and she found them, and she got to tell them that she had seen Jesus, and He was alive! All her pain and shame were gone, replaced by the hope of His resurrection.

Sometimes we go through stuff—hard stuff, unfair stuff, and painful stuff. Sometimes it lasts a long time, and we get tired or lonely, or start to lose hope, or deal with depression or anxiety from it. Sometimes it creates shame in our lives, even when it's not our own fault. And all we want to do is just see His face and hear from Him. We just need to know He will show up for us in the "tombs of life." And if we wait, and rest, and trust, He *will* show up. But sometimes it can feel like we got an unfair amount of pain from unfair circumstances. And there is just no time to deal with it.

Sometimes we need, in the middle of our pain, to just stop, kneel, and cry out to Him: "I need to see You, Lord. Where are You? Will You please show Your face to me? I just need to see You, because what I'm going through just doesn't seem to make sense!" We need to honestly cry out to Him and ask Him to roll the stone away from our hearts. The stone may be in the shape of shame—or hate, or unforgiveness, or clinging to pain, or doubt, or fear, or addiction. These stones block our hearts from seeing Him and His resurrection in our own lives. And when that happens, the journey and the process can become a story of redemption and hope, glorifying His resurrection power, and providing the kind of healing only He can give.

Then we are to use it to help others—to run and tell others, sort of like Mary did, that "He is risen and alive ... I have seen Him ... and I will never be the same!"

CHAPTER 8

Letting Go of Lost Loved Ones

"**I**T'S NOT YOUR JOB," THE FAMILIAR VOICE WHISPERED. IT WAS A VOICE I'D heard many times—inaudible, but one that unmistakably came to the heart of my soul. One that came to me again, after worrying, fretting, trying to fix the situation, and finally praying over choices a loved one was making. And then a conversation began in my mind and heart. (I have used the "he" pronoun for consistency, but please feel free to switch it to the "she" you may be concerned about as well.)

"It's not your job to make sure he follows Me. That's my job. I'm the shepherd. And I am really pretty good at it! And I know my sheep."

"But Father God, he's lost. He's not following you, and he's going to run off a cliff, and I need to run after him, because I don't want him to get hurt. And if I can just get him to turn around and look at You, he'll see what a good shepherd You are!"

"My dear daughter, I know exactly where he is. And I will always go after my stray sheep. I am not taking a vacation from my job. And besides, doesn't your head hurt a little bit?"

"My head, Father? What do you mean?"

"Well, I thought your head might hurt, because you keep running into the fence that I put up to protect you and the other sheep. It's my way of loving you with a healthy boundary, you know, so you don't get hurt!"

"Well, I have had some pain, I guess—sleepless nights, headaches, distraction from worrying so much. And my shoulders have really been aching lately, and my neck has this crick in it. I guess it's from feeling the heaviness of the yolk I've been carrying. It's hard to carry someone else's life and welfare on my shoulders! But my intentions are so good! I keep running into the fence, because I'm trying to get him to follow You, and that is hard work! That is what You want, right?"

"Yes, I want him to follow Me. But your job is not to push him or try to get him to do anything. It's just to follow Me, as well. And to tell Me about him."

"But Father, he's so lost. I'm just trying to help! But I am tired—actually, I'm exhausted—and what I'm doing just does not seem to be working. And I really need a massage or something because this yolk is just killing me! It's just too heavy for me!

"Yes, I bet it is! That's why I am reminding you that it's My job to lead my sheep. I never push. And I will always know where he is. He's never out of my sight. He just needs to see that the pasture he's in will not provide what he's looking for. When he gets hungry enough, he will look for Me. And I will be there to lead him back to the flock. So, you can quit butting your head up against the fence. I've got this. But thanks for caring so much about him. And if you start worrying about him again, you can always talk to Me. I know it's hard for you to wait sometimes! And about that yolk thing—why don't you just take it off? It does not fit you. I'm not sure why you thought it did, because it was perfectly designed for Me. I can handle the responsibility for your loved one's life. How about you just love him, and I will save him? I've been waiting for you to let go of that heavy burden and lean on me. Here, take my hand."

"Okay, I think I'm getting it now. I'm not his shepherd; I'm just a fellow sheep. My head is starting to feel better already! And taking off this yolk thing is really starting to feel good! I bet I've even lost a few pounds. I feel so much lighter! I think I'll do a little stretching or sheep yoga, because my muscles have been aching for soooo long. I didn't realize the strain that burden was putting on my body, mind, and spirit. I guess you already know that us sheep are not always the smartest animals in the pen, sorry! Then I am going to lie down by Your feet for a while if that's okay. Thanks. It sure is peaceful here!"

"That is good, My daughter. It's exactly where I want you! And you really do not need to move for a while; just rest. Like I said, I've got this. And I can see your loved one; he's not too far away to ever be out of My sight. I'll keep watch over him and protect him while he's wandering around out there. And I'll call out his name every so often too, so he hears my voice and remembers the way back home, inside the fence. My sheep never forget the sound of My voice, even though sometimes they play hide-and-seek from Me. It's kind of funny that they think I don't see them! I've had some who got so lost in the woods and the thickets that they couldn't have found their way home on their own, and because they wandered too far away from the safe, fenced pasture—and got pretty banged up. And that is when I have gone out and gathered them up in My arms and carried them home. And then I take care of them, and they are always so grateful. And, boy, are they hungry—ready to eat a horse— except for the vegetarians, of course! Ha-ha, that was a Creator joke! They love to graze the green grass in the pasture that I keep in good shape, just waiting for them. And they sometimes must learn to be around the other sheep again and play nicely, because they're used to butting their heads, just for survival out there."

"Wow, Father, You really are a wise and good Shepherd. I had no idea! I really thought I was helping You by running after him, and I just love him so much, and don't want to see him go through all that suffering, like what You just told me. I wish he knew just how much I don't want to see him get hurt. Do You know what I mean? I just wish he knew how much I love him!"

"Yes, my daughter, I know exactly what you mean. My Son Jesus and I talk about that all the time. We've got that covered too. He knows that is why I had to send Him and why I had to watch Him suffer, for things He did not even do. I understand what it means to love so much that we hurt when our loved ones hurt and make bad choices and turn away from our love for them. It cost my Son His life! But we're together now, and Jesus tells me all the time about how hard it is for all of you to live around so much evil and pain on the earth. He was just asking me today to keep special watch over you and your loved one. And He just beamed when He talked about when you both will be here with us, and how much you're going to love it!"

"Wow, Father, I never really got this concept before. Thanks so much! I think I can rest much better now. But I'll have to reorganize my time a little bit. That worrying and fixing filled up my mental planner, more than I realized. I'm going to have a lot more time and energy on my hands, now. Maybe I'll get myself back in shape! I bet I could even start running again and not be weary. What do You think?"

"That would make Me really happy. I love it when my children take care of the treasure of themselves, and let me take care of all their loved ones in the ways that only I can do! And one more thing. You can come to Me anytime and tell Me more about your loved one. I love hearing from you! And remember that I love him even more than you do, although I know that's hard for you to understand. I wrote that in my love letter to you. Why don't you go read it again? It just might help. Good talk, My daughter, good talk!"

CHAPTER 9

Letting Go of Fearing the Future

A STORM WAS ROLLING IN. I KNEW, BECAUSE I HAD A PERFECT VANTAGE point to hear the northeast Kansas thunder roll in on that hot, sultry August evening. My spot to watch the storm slowly make its entry was perfect! I needed a getaway—to write, rest, walk, and pray. After thirteen months of nonstop drama and trauma that had been a mental, physical, and emotional challenge, I needed to seek out a "happy place" where I could just "be." So, I came to a Christian retreat center called Living Waters Ranch, hidden in the Flint Hills of northeastern Kansas, overlooking a very large, peaceful reservoir and beautiful rolling hills. It has been my hideaway off and on for four decades, at times in life that have always seemed to involve some sort of crossroads. You know those times—when you need escape from activity, or people, or decisions, or you just want to enjoy nature and no technology. The times when the big question of "What's next?" has loomed so large that daily routines and familiarity need to disappear, and the simplicity of a room with a bed, and lots of open space to walk, think, and pray became a welcome sanctuary. For me, the questions have revolved around life changes. What's next after college? What's next after full-time youth ministry? What's next after marriage, children, and an unexpected divorce? What's next after ten years of single parenting and fourteen years of being single again? And I was there again, asking God, "What's next after four years of a new marriage, blended family, and the age of sixty rushing at me like a freight train without an engineer?"

So, after a day full of Kansas August sunshine and ninety-degree heat, the evening sunset painted the sky with beautiful red, orange, and yellow strokes, ending hours of hiking to the top of a hill to soak it all in. Just three hours before, not a cloud was in the sky, and the only sound was of the soft drone of motorboats and Jet Skis, humming their way through the end of summer. But then, with the locusts singing their evening lullaby, the big clouds gathering, the lightning flashes striking across the darkening sky, and the faint sound of thunder's distant rumble, I heard nature announcing that a storm was definitely coming! Being a Midwestern native, the emotions were the same that I've had my whole life when one of these storms moves in. There's a mixture of awe at the rapidly changing skyline, a healthy respect and caution at knowing what damage these storms can do, and a warm feeling inside of memories of storms decades of summers ago as a little girl, learning from my dad how to not get scared during them. He would tell me to watch the lightning, then count the seconds until hearing the thunder. Every time, it worked. My focus shifted from fear to focusing on counting, and a sort of delight when the thunder would boom, right at about five to eight seconds, and I was amazed at how smart my daddy was! As this storm moved in, I was still in awe of the night beauty as the lightning suddenly painted a dark canvas with jagged flashes of brilliant white, each different from the last strike. And there was still a little healthy fear, which came from adult eyes that have experienced the aftermath of damage from tornadoes and severe thunderstorms that twisted cars into trees, pushed trees into homes, and created flooded basements and streets.

I wondered about this storm, like I often wonder about the future, and "What's next?" Would this just get the area really wet, or would it be worse than that? Would my car be okay parked under that tree, or would the tree be *in* my car when I saw it in the morning? Would things look different tomorrow, or would they be recognizable? It's the same with the future. We watch the storms of life roll in, oftentimes right after a really good day or experience. And then it begins. The clouds of life start forming. The phone rings with the unexpected news of a loved one dying or with a diagnosis that just wasn't in our plans. And we did not even see the lightning strike. It was just like a sudden clap of thunder—*bam!* Another friend, or maybe you, are heading for a divorce that you just never thought would happen. *Flash!* More lightning! The unknown horizon of tomorrow includes wondering if maybe you'll finally hear from the rebellious son or daughter who is choosing to go down a path causing a wake of tornado-like destruction to them and everyone who loves them. *Flash, bam!* The seconds between their choices and consequences are so close they can't even be counted. But one thing that anyone who grows up in the Midwest knows how to do when the news flashes the severe weather alerts is to heed the warnings to "take cover!" It's instinctual, especially if you have been around a few years; you take shelter in a basement or room with no windows. You have your supplies ready—a flashlight, blankets, battery-operated radio, and bottles of water. And shoes are important, so that you don't step on debris and broken glass if the storm does do damage. Even with all the warnings, though, more than one person has tragically lost their life because of not heeding those warnings, thinking they could just run outside and get a quick glance at the funnel cloud, or try to drive across a flooded road. They just did not heed the warnings, thinking they could face the storm alone and unguarded, only to reap the sad consequences of that misjudgment.

Sometimes we do the same with life's storms—not heeding the warnings—and then having to recover from the aftermath. Wanting to ease loneliness of singleness, so not heeding the red flags in a deceptive relationship, until severe damage has been done. Making a purchase without funds in the bank, which created unnecessary long-term debt. Speaking too quickly or in anger, causing damage to a relationship with a loved one. I am in that human camp. However, there are times that I have heeded warnings—either from those who loved me enough to confront me, or from the still, quiet voice I've come to recognize as being from a wise heavenly Father who gently reminds me that His way is better than mine. And at those times, disaster has been avoided, unnecessary hurt and pain have been preempted, and my heart and life, or that of my loved ones, has been protected. The amazing thing about taking cover in the shelter of God's loving arms and words of warning through the storms of life is that tomorrow's "what ifs" lose their punch of fear. And even in those times when I haven't heeded His warnings, His grace has always provided a way through the aftermath of my self-will, setting me back on the path He's ordained for me. He is so eager to do that for us if our hearts are truly repentant and turned toward Him. Sometimes the debris from our decisions takes a while to clean up, just like after a bad storm. I saw a town devastated several years ago from an F4 tornado, where blocks and blocks of homes, trees, vehicles, and memories were splintered into nothing. It took a few years, but now that place of former devastation boasts beautiful new homes, growing trees, and lives that picked up and went on, once the mess was cleaned up. The morning after that tornado brought the shock of "Now what?" to so many people and families who wondered how they would be able to function or get back to normal lives again.

But they all have—some relocating, and some rebuilding in the same spot. God helps us do that also. Sometimes we must change a lot around us, and sometimes we just need a heart change, after surviving life's storms. But it's always possible, and it starts with choosing to release the fear of the unknown that our hands grasp so tightly and grab the hand of the One who picks us up after the storm, helps us clean up the debris in our hearts and lives, and places us back on living life moment by moment and day by day.

The thunder and light display subsided in the storm that summer night, and the rain came and went. No tornado, no storm damage, just a wetter ground and cooler temperature aiding a good night's sleep. The next morning my car was in the same place and was treeless! The next day transitioned from being the future to the present, and the journey of life began again. And I have continued to face more mornings of beautiful sunshine as well as troubling times of loss and heartache. But I've been able to face whatever is coming, because I've seen God carry me through life's storms and transitions repeatedly. He is my shelter, and He can be yours, no matter what! We can smile at the future and not be paralyzed with fear because eventually the sun always comes out again.

CHAPTER 10

Letting Go
Because Of Grief

I BEGAN WRITING THIS BOOK, AND THIS CHAPTER, ABOUT SIX YEARS AGO, never imagining that life's major interruptions would put off finishing my efforts for so long. And I never imagined that we would lose three family members, plus several close friends mostly within the last eleven months, and all since the pandemic started twenty months ago. What I initially wrote about letting go of loved ones, now seems so much different than in this post COVID-19 year of loss after loss. The week of March 8-13, 2021, was the one year anniversary of when the NBA shut down, when the strange sickness that was starting to affect people was a huge bubble of questions, and also when we got a phone call that rocked our world. And then another phone call happened on Dec. 17, nine months later. The first call was the beginning of a surreal journey of the next four and a half days of making a nine-hour trip to Colorado and walking into a hospital room where my dear sister-in-law Nancy was laying unresponsive, after a stroke. The second phone call was from my own sister, instigating a rushed two-hour trip to go be by my Mother's side, in her full care home. I watched both of those amazing, wonderful women take their last breaths, nine months apart, as Heaven opened its doors to welcome them to their forever homes. And I will never be the same. Nancy was the first sibling of my husband's that I met, and we got along well instantly...common views of life, common love and concern about adult children, and a common love of laughter, faith, and view of the realities of life and family. She quickly became more than a sister-in-law for our marriage that began when we were both fifty-four years old... she became a trusted friend.

And then there was Mom. She had lived a life of tragedy, joy, challenges, and quiet faith in her ninety-six-and-a-half years like no one else I have ever known. We all knew her last few years had been "bonus years", as we watched dementia, hearing and eyesight loss affect her with each visit. Our family had moved her from her longtime home of fifty-one years, after a couple of years of discussion, lots of prayer, and more than gentle urging. She finally agreed, after a night of prayer and feeling like "something told me I need to do this". She went from an independent living apartment in a retirement center, to a full care home during her last three years. It was in the same town as my sister and brother-in-law, who kept her company a couple of times a week and were available to help with many things like errands and medical appointments. None of us expected the COVID-19 virus, and how it would affect our last year of life with her. My monthly visits for the four hour round trip, became much more complicated, as the visits had to be from an outside patio, with a mask on, basically yelling, so she could hear me from inside her care home. The visits that I used to spend most of the day doing, including eating lunch with her, turned into about one-and-a-half hours, which was all she could handle, and my trips home included pulling over to sob and pray, so that I could safely drive the two hours back home. My two adult sons, her only grandchildren, had six hour round trips to make, and since their industries were both drastically affected by the COVID-19 virus, their trips were also limited and difficult emotionally. So, my Mom-heart was also carrying their emotional pain, especially knowing how hard it was on them when Mom (Grandma) started getting us confused with other family members toward the end. It was gut-wrenching. The patio visits turned into masked visits through her bedroom window, after she was moved into a Hospice bed. It was tough on the whole family, but we were so thankful that we could see her and talk to her privately. The last visit like that was on an unusually warm and sunny December day, so my husband and I could stay by her window a little longer. She asked again why we could not come inside, which had been happening for the entire ten months of pandemic lockdown, and I explained once again. She said, "Well...it's a crazy world out there!" I agreed, and we laughed together. That would be my last conversation with her. A few days later, my Sister, Brother-in-law, husband, and myself, were given a gift of being able to rotate visits with her during her last twenty four hours on earth, in her room, without masks, to be able to say goodbye as she was released from a tired and hurting earthly body into her Heavenly home. That gift is something I will cling to, after not being able to touch her or be near her for nearly a year...for the rest of my life. I am still in the first year of grieving this woman who was with me my entire life, from the beginning of being formed in her womb. I am also grieving the loss of not being able to be with her for most of the last year of her life, due to a horrible pandemic that has taken the lives of millions of people and caused illness in many more millions. Some of my friends have been among those who were not able to be with their elderly parents at all during their COVID-19 caused deaths, and I hurt for them as well.

Three short months after my Mom's death, my Mother-in-law's health also took a downhill turn, and we lost her on March 25th, 2021. After a surreal series of quick decisions and an emergency surgery, this wonderful woman also passed into her eternal home. She was a gift to me, after meeting and marrying Ed at age fifty-four, and she welcomed me and my grown sons into her life and heart from the very beginning. Since we were the only of her family who lived in the same town, spending time with her became a weekly part of my life, and her quick wit and deep faith were huge blessings to me, and to many others. Her absence is felt in a palpable way, and we are both still reeling from the reality of losing both Moms within three months of each other. Our home quickly filled with family and overnight company for nine days, and a funeral was planned for two days later, due to most of the family members already having arrived from out of state. During the last difficult days of Mom Betty's life, Bridget, who had been a teenager in the youth group I had been a director for in the early 1980's, also passed away, while waiting for a lung transplant. Three weeks later I was again in the operating room, this time for hernia surgery.

It was just a few weeks after that surgery that Clarence, another dear soul, and who was like a second father to me, also passed into his Heavenly home. In the few months since then, several more friends lost family members. So, as I write this, my mind, body, and spirit are still reeling and healing from loss after loss and change after change. Simply put, there is nothing easy about losing loved ones and dealing with the memories, dreams, and sudden bursts of emotion triggered by some little reminder that came out of the blue. And there is nothing easy about life going on as though everything is the same, when nothing is the same, nor will it ever be. I am also realizing that loss after loss with no break, can create a state of being in perpetual grief. The grief cycle of denial, anger, bargaining, depression, and acceptance is a roller coaster I've been on for several months, feeling like a hamster in a wheel. Every time I thought I was getting off, there was another death, forcing me to push through all of the stages again. But I know I have to go through the stages in order to heal, after many years of learning that losing our loved ones is a part of the circle of life. And grief is the price of loving and losing someone who will always have a part of our hearts.

The reality of death first came when I was in Jr. High, and losing a beautiful, active cheerleader friend suddenly, due to spinal meningitis. We were all at such a tender age, trying to begin to figure out who we were as early adolescents, getting interested in the opposite sex, going to basketball games and beginning the crowd mentality of our peers becoming more important (and more fun!), than our parents. Death was not on our radar, especially of this vibrant girl, Deanna, who cheered at a game on Friday night, developed strange symptoms, and was gone from us by Saturday night. I remember feeling like a truck of reality had hit me right in the face...that there are no guarantees of how long we have on this earth. That unexpected and unimaginable things can happen within twenty-four hours that we have no control over, that can change a life, a family, and an entire class of seventh graders from a small central Kansas town. It was a life-changing moment for me, realizing that I might not live to an old age, and that my life decisions, even in early adolescence, were kind of a big deal. It was the beginning of my search about what comes after death, and how would I know whether Heaven was for real or not...and especially how I would know I would be there, rather than the place called hell that I'd heard about growing up in church. We all had to grow up a little bit quicker because of losing Deanna.

There is a piece of paper that I have saved for several years, which is a funeral program of Sally, another friend who died after one year of cancer. She also was very special, and one of our last conversations together was about how she was looking forward to "dancing with Jesus" when she passed from this earth, although our conversation turned to concerns for the loved ones she was leaving behind. There is a picture of her smiling her big, beautiful smile on the front of that program, and I decided to keep it in the front of my Bible. Many times, since then, opening my Bible for answers, peace, wisdom, comfort, or joy, I have first seen the picture of Sally...and can almost hear her whisper, "Just wait, Noreen!! You won't believe it here...it's AWESOME, and I got to dance with Jesus again today!" I can't tell you how many times that has helped with recovery from medical appointments as well as life's disappointments...or just on the days I feel joy and thankfulness, and then remember that all of what we experience here on earth is really so temporary in the greater scheme of things.

There have been many other loved ones whose presence and lives I miss dearly...some who passed many years ago, and some not so long ago. My Dad has been gone for eighteen years now, and there are still some days that I long for one more conversation with him, or to hear him tell just one more joke with his slow, deep voice. The causes of death of family and friends have included cancer, car accidents, suicides, a brain aneurysm, pneumonia, AIDS, and most shockingly, murder. Losing loved ones is one of life's most difficult challenges, whether we know it's coming, or a total, life-shattering shock. There's no easy or perfect way to grieve, and there's certainly no timeline that is a "one size fits all" solution. The letting go process can be a roller-coaster unparalleled to anything else we experience in life, with periods of doing ok, only to have an unexpected trigger trip our emotions in a way that brings memories in a burst similar to a fireworks display on 4th of July! As I continue this journey on earth, and sixty-five birthdays have come and gone, I'm more convinced than ever that the only salve for the pain of having to let go of our loved ones is hanging on to the One who made them and us. Some of them, it feels, have been snatched out of our hands with no warning or preparation. And some have been slowly released over a long-term disease or many decades of just having a worn-out body that's ready for eternal rest. In either case, letting go of our grip on them, our desire to keep them in our lives, and our mass of emotions that accompany the loss of them, is anything but simple. I don't have any easy answers for how that should happen, or the timeline, but I have come to experience that letting go of loved ones is much easier if we open our empty hands that miss holding and hugging them, and reach for the hand of God's comfort, trusting Him with the unanswered questions of a life lost to us... and let Him hold and hug us.

Grief, and the process of grief, seems to not fit into our world today of everything being available at the click of a mouse or a cell phone or tablet. It's not in our planners or our goals or our life-coaching mentoring. It's painful and difficult and confusing, and you can google a million ways to do it but walking through it in real life is still an unavoidable necessity. It can create disappointment from others who say well-meaning, but absolutely not helpful, things to try to ease or speed up our process, because they are terribly uncomfortable watching us hurt. It's all too easy to want to "fix" someone else's loss, rather than just being there for the long haul, making ourselves available to them in whatever way is needed. Our busy, over-planned lives are often not easily adjusted to finding a new normal that has a huge gap in which a loved one used to dwell. A few days after losing Mom, helping plan a long-distance memorial service, then going through surgery ten days later, my grief rushed to the top like an oil well with a gusher. The sounds coming out of me were not cries, they were deep, guttural wails that I just could not stop. And I let them rip, knowing that it was a horrible, but necessary part of getting through all the loss and pain and reality...and that trying to stop it would only delay the inevitable. My husband heard me from another floor of the house, and came beside me, put his hand on my shoulder, and didn't say a word. He stood there in that manner, until I finally stopped, and that is the best thing he could have done at that time. I didn't need any words, I didn't even need a hug, I just needed his hand on my shoulder. He knew that, because he had gone through his own losses, before losing his sister. He had lost his first wife to a long battle with cancer, he had lost his dad to ALS, and he had lost two close friends, who were also brothers to each other…all within four years before he met me. Like in any situation, people who have gone through losses of loved ones are oftentimes the only ones who can empathize and comfort in the ways that are needed and most helpful.

Jesus went through losing loved ones too. There were two sisters and a brother, who were friends of His. They shared a friendship with Him and believed in His ability to perform miracles. When the brother, named Lazarus, died, Jesus was not even in the same town. There were no text messages or social media for sisters Mary and Martha to reach Him by. They couldn't pick up the phone and tell Him that their beloved brother, His friend, was gone. They had already sent word to Jesus telling Him that Lazarus was sick, thinking He would show up quickly. But He didn't leave the town He was in for two more days. So by the time He arrived, Lazarus had been dead for four days, in a tomb, wrapped in burial rags of that day and time, and Mary and Martha had all of the shock and unanswered questions we all struggle with, as to why their brother had died. They also struggled with the question of where Jesus was and why it took Him so long to get there. They wanted Jesus to prevent the death of their beloved one. They didn't understand why it had to happen, and one of the sisters was more than a little upset when Jesus arrived, saying, "Lord, if you had been here, my brother would not have died." (John 11:21 NIV). That was Martha…the busy one, who always tried to keep everything running and in order. She asked of the Savior the question so many of us have (or want to) ask, when the loss of someone we love, or someone we've heard of on the news, seems to go so much earlier than what we think should have happened. She wasn't without faith, because she knew that Jesus had the power to keep her beloved brother from dying…and it just didn't make sense to her, it didn't fit into her timeline of what should have happened. And in her grief and confusion, she even acknowledged that Jesus was the Messiah…. but then she stopped the conversation and went and got her sister, Mary. I wonder if she left in anger or had to get back to whatever task at hand, or just couldn't deal with what she didn't understand. For whatever reason, it seemed best to just get her sister to take over talking with the Son of God.

Enter Mary, who was told that Jesus had finally arrived. Mary...the one who loved sitting at Jesus' feet, soaking up what He said, and who could have often been the only woman among the male followers of Jesus. She was weeping when she ran out to meet Him, and she said the same thing her sister had said, "Lord, if you had been here, my brother would not have died" (John 11:32 NIV). And this time, He was deeply moved and troubled, and asked where Lazarus had been laid. So, Mary and her friends, who from Biblical account again seem to be men, took Him to the tomb where Lazarus had been put. But by then, Jesus wept. I think He wept, because He saw their sorrow, and knew he would be seeing his friend dead. I also think that it was to let them, and us, know that crying in the face of losing a loved one, is just a part of the process. Maybe it was because He saw Mary weeping, and it's interesting that there was no mention of Martha weeping. Both sisters loved and were in grief over their brother dying, but my guess is the difference was in their attitudes and personalities. Martha was busy and seemed mad and accusatory. She confronted Jesus about His absence, then left. After all, she had lots to do! Maybe feeding guests who had come to grieve her brother, maybe keeping busy to avoid her own grief and loss, or maybe because she felt she had to double-time the household duties because her sister wasn't doing anything, in her opinion. In our day, Martha might be labeled as obsessive-compulsive or a control freak, and it's possible that her sister would be considered the "too-sensitive" one, or co-dependent, or maybe even lazy. It's so easy to be critical of someone else's reaction to grief and loss, when it doesn't fit into the way we process it! Truth is, there is no perfect way. When Jesus saw the tomb, He told them to roll away the stone! Of course, Martha would be the one who would object. She reminded her friend Jesus, the Son of God, that there would be an odor, a BAD odor. After all, her beloved brother's body had been in there, wrapped up in burial linens, without our modern-day embalming fluids or air conditioning, for four days! Maybe she was trying to figure out how to "clean" the smell, somehow feeling responsible for that also. Mary was just caught up in the moment, probably amazed at what she already sensed would be happening because she knew Jesus was *there*.

For whatever reason, the smell seemed more important at the time than the fact that Jesus had just told all of them that they would see the glory of God, so that they'd believe He was sent by God. Then Jesus raised Lazarus from the dead, and he came out of the tomb with his hands and feet still wrapped with strips of linen, and a burial cloth around his face!! He told the Jewish friends of Mary to "Take off the grave clothes and let him go." (John 11:44 NIV). I can almost see Martha dropping her handful of cleaning supplies, and Mary dropping to her knees, both reacting in disbelief, and yet huge relief! Their brother was alive again, and that's all that mattered!! Their story ended in a way all of us who have lost loved ones would love to experience. Most of us, with rare exception, do not get to have our loved ones return from the dead, although there are stories of someone coming back to life after several minutes of death, which is as amazing as four days to our modern-day minds. Those who follow Jesus, have the comfort of knowing that their loved one who followed Jesus is in Heaven, and that they will one day be reunited, which can soften the loss, of course. And the difficulty of losing someone who's place in eternity is a big question mark, can also be softened with the choice to believe that God is all-knowing, as well as merciful and just. They are where they should be, and God is the only one who truly knows a person's heart and all that happens in their last thoughts and breaths. He is the only one who may be present when someone turns to Him, or returns to Him, in their final moments on earth. When I have struggled with the death of someone whom I'm not sure I will be seeing in eternity, I remember my friend who came from a simple background, and his theology is also simple, and yet profound. We were in a group discussion about current events at the time and cultural issues and lifestyle choices of people and the resulting effect on their destination after death. He summed it up by saying "They'll know when they get there", and I just burst out laughing! There was nothing more accurate and truer that could have brought the lively discussion to a sudden halt. God's wisdom, God's mercy, God's justice, and God's redemption are all enveloped in the sacrifice of Jesus, and the availability of eternity with Him. And each person gets to choose whether they believe that or not, so we can let go of the unknown in those situations and grasp His hand of comfort.

The whole scenario with Martha and Mary is like ours when we must let a loved one go. Some of us get busy with the difficult tasks at hand, and some of us just weep, and some of us comfort others. It's all a part of the process of grief that is inevitable, and just doesn't seem to always fit into a perfect little box. It's called "acceptance" in the grief cycle. Sometimes it takes weeks, or years, or even decades, depending on how the loss happened. But the one thing we do have control over is our attitude about the loss. We get to choose to become bitter or better. Clinging to the unfairness or trusting God's sovereignty in the midst of our pain. Clutching our anger and own schedules of what events we think our own particular universe should include, or opening our tear-stained, grief-wrecked hearts and hands to Him. Not being afraid to cry out to Him," If you just would have been there, he or she wouldn't have died... where were you??" And He will be moved and weep with you and hold you while you weep and question. And eventually, you can sense your hand in His, in fact maybe you will sense that He was holding you in the palm of His hand all along, and that even in your grief, you will somehow see God. It may be by using your experience to help someone else who never got to bring their baby home from the hospital either. Or joining a grief support group. Or helping to get laws passed to prevent alcohol-related deaths. Or participating in a cancer awareness walk. These things won't necessarily take away all of the questions, or the painful feelings of anniversary dates, but they can help soften the sting.

A hand clutched around unresolved grief will not allow the healing necessary to be opened to life continuing. A hand opened to clutching the hand of the same Jesus who wept over losing His friend, will allow grief to do its job, and find life on the other side. It's not easy, or comfortable, but it is possible. And then we can finally hear His voice tell us, like he told Mary, to "take off the grave clothes and let him go" (John 11:44 NIV). This does not mean we forget them or avoid memories of them. Instead it means that life, although altered forever by our loss, starts beginning again, one minute and one day at a time. Sometimes that may include counseling, a doctor's care, or just honest talks with safe people in our lives who are willing to come alongside us, to listen, cry and pray for us as we process the myriad of emotions that at times can be shocking and confusing. One thing I can say without hesitation is that Jesus is very near to the brokenhearted. He understands our grief. He understands our broken hearts. He understands our pain, like no human being can. He is there in the middle of the night, in the middle of the tears, and in the middle of the fog of figuring life out without our loved ones. He even understands if you're angry at Him and can handle you telling him that. He understands the cost of love, because His love for us caused Him to die for you and for me. Let Him love you, and let others help you. I am not alone in my grief, and neither are you.

CHAPTER 11

He's Got You!

WHEN I HAD THE OPPORTUNITY TO GO TO HAITI FOR A SHORT-TERM mission trip, it was to help with children in an orphanage. There was a group of us, including my husband and several family members. That country had gone through a horrific earthquake four years before, killing and displacing hundreds of thousands of people. Many of the children we met still had living parents but were put in the orphanage because earthquake damage robbed the parents of being able to provide for their children. I was amazed at how something as small as a bottle of bubbles brought squeals of laughter from the little ones who shared large rooms with many beds, and every meal with scores of other children. Toward the end of our time there, the highlight was loading all of them up in trucks and vans and taking them to the beach. Although this beach was nothing like a resort area or vacation destination, we were all ready to jump into the water and just watch the children splash and jump into the waves.

One little boy seemed to be at home in the water, and I thought it would be fun to teach him to float. So, I convinced him to lay his back on my hands and feel the security of knowing I was holding him up with my hands just below the water's surface. Then I gradually lowered my hands, coaching him to stick his belly up high, but he immediately panicked and started sinking. I put my hands back under his back and calmly said I was still there. We repeated this scenario over and over, each time with me letting go of him a little longer. When this little guy would start to sink, he would say in broken English, "You got me?" And I would reply, "I got you. Don't worry, I'm still here." Each time, he would stay afloat on his own a little longer, staring into my eyes for the reassurance that I wasn't going to let him sink. And finally, this little boy who had lost so much security from a life devastated by tragedy, realized he could trust me and quit panicking. He started floating on his own and was thrilled at being able to accomplish such a feat!

Fear is the enemy of trust. And if we have gone through betrayal, or prayers not being answered the way we asked, or not being convinced that God really loves us, that can create fear in trusting Him. We can feel like He has let go of us and do not realize that His hands are still there holding us, keeping us from drowning in the middle of a mess. Many times, I've been overwhelmed with a situation or desired change and have cried out to Him like my little water-loving friend did to me. And when I look to Him instead of the waters of life raging around me, I've been reassured with scriptures like, "So do not fear, for I am with you; do not be dismayed, for I am your God. I will strengthen you and help you; I will uphold you with my righteous right hand" (Isaiah 41:10 NIV). When my eyes are fixed on Him, I will not drown, but when I take things into my own hands, I begin to sink. And if I remember that He held me up the last time, I quit flailing on my own, and rest in knowing that He's got me!

The problem with learning this kind of trust is that it usually comes in an exceedingly difficult time, when my own resources and efforts have been depleted. And none of us like those times. We love to see God provide and pull us up out of the waves of life, but the process of getting to that point is no fun when we are in the middle of it. But with each time of seeing God provide, rescue, and love me back to the other side of a challenge, I am learning to rest in His arms a little longer. And resting in His arms means letting go—of control, of creating my own ending, and of the need to understand the big question of "Why?" We cannot grab His hand in trust, with a clenched fist. Release can only come when every finger is open to what He has in store, knowing that He still has us, and He's not going to let us drown. Sometimes it requires gut-level honesty of admitting we are not sure if He is there for us. Sometimes it requires tears, the release of getting back at someone, or accepting a physical setback or diagnosis. Sometimes it requires a difficult talk with someone, or professional counseling. And all the time, it requires faith that He really is there for us, even in the struggle of not understanding the situation we're in. It's when words like "Never will I leave you; never will I forsake you" (Hebrews 13:5 NIV) jump off the page of the Bible and become a lifeline, keeping us afloat.

I will be the first to admit that this letting go process can be hard—even excruciating at times. And oftentimes it can take much longer than I want it to. Learning to unclench a fist of control and trust God seems so against what can often make sense to us. But when we let go, we also receive what He has in His hand to give us. When unforgiveness is released, His amazing grace and forgiveness of us can be grasped. When control of someone else's life is released, His sovereign and good will for that person can be accepted, as we continue to be vessels of love in their life. When a job is lost or left, we can be redirected to His provision and protection for our lives. And when worry is released, peace and joy in knowing we do not have to carry the weight of the world on our shoulders allows us to let God have His job back! His provision is worth the process, and He is ready and waiting for each of us to let go and grasp His hand. My prayer for you is that this book has been an encouragement to begin to let go of what you've been holding onto so tightly that it's been holding you back from getting to experience God's presence, peace, and faithfulness.

Are you ready to unclench your fist, and open your hand to grasp His? If so, take a minute to begin that process now. Open your hands out before you, one finger at a time, as you name each situation, person, heartache, loss, life change, or anything else to which you have clung. Take your time and ask God to show you if there is anything else. Then with opened hands, fingers flat and spread out, take a long breath, and imagine all those things being released into God's faithful care of you, His treasured child. And then imagine God's hand lovingly grasping yours and filling you with love, peace, and release that can only come from Him. When you feel a tendency to regrasp what you just let go of, remember this exercise and your decision to release it. And when there is a new scenario that you find yourself tightening your grip around, do the exercise again. Letting go is a lifetime journey because we're human beings, constantly influenced by fear and control. Discovering God's faithfulness by our letting go can change the trajectory of our lives and the generations who come after us toward peace, health, and wholeness. From a fellow traveler on this journey, may you be blessed as you unclench your fists.